TATE COLLECTION

The Tate collection is owned by the nation. It is the national collection of British art from 1500 to the present, and of modern and contemporary art from around the world.

TATE GALLERIES

There are four Tate Galleries across the country. In London, Tate Britain specialises in British art, while Tate Modern shows international modern and contemporary art. Tate Liverpool also focuses on modern and contemporary art, while Tate St Ives displays work related to the area and the artists who worked there.

INTERNATIONAL

Since Tate Modern opened in 2000, the collection has become more global. A broader selection of work has been acquired from areas such as Latin America, Middle East and North Africa, South Asia, Russia and Eastern Europe, and Asia-Pacific.

NEW TATE MODERN

OPENS 17 JUNE 2016

ART CHANGES

The collection has expanded in other ways, as artist themselves find new ways of working. There is a greater emphasis on large-scale installations, the projected image, and performance-based work. Photography has also become an important element of the collection.

NEW TATE MODERN

In response to the changing nature of the collection, a new ten-storey extension to Tate Modern opened in June 2016. The increased space enables the gallery to highlight developments in art over the last few decades, and explore the networks of influence and communication linking artists around the world.

TATE HISTORY

The Tate galleries are named after Henry Tate, a Victorian businessman who made his fortune through refining sugar and manufacturing sugar cubes. He was also one of Britain's most important art collectors.

In 1889 he offered to donate his collection to the nation on the condition that a suitable gallery was built to display it. Constructed on the site of a recently demolished prison, the National Gallery of British Art at Millbank opened to the public in 1897. Seven rooms were added to house the substantial collection of works bequeathed by J.M.W. Turner. There was a further expansion in the 1920s to show international modern and contemporary art as well as British art. In 1932 the gallery was officially renamed as the Tate Gallery, and was recognised as an independent institution in 1955.

Tate began to grow beyond a single gallery in the 1980s. A new site was chosen in Liverpool to focus on modern art. Designed by James Stirling, it was located in a disused warehouse on the Albert Dock. Completed in May 1988, Tate Liverpool attracts more than 60,000 visitors each year.

Postcard view of Tate Gallery, Millbank, in 1907

The Turbine Hall before redevelopment

With the opening of Tate Modern in 2000, the former Tate Gallery was renamed Tate Britain and returned to its original role as a centre for British art. Tate Modern itself has been a remarkable success, drawing in more than 40 million visitors, becoming the most popular museum of modern art in the world, and helping to rejuvenate Bankside as a tourist destination.

These unprecedented visitor figures, along with the changing nature of contemporary art, have underlined the need to expand the gallery, with new designs by Herzog & de Meuron. The first phase of the project was the conversion of the former oil tanks as a space for live art and the projected image. In June 2016 the Switch House was completed, with new exhibition, learning, retail and refreshment spaces. The new extension allows Tate Modern to show art from a wider geographical range, more ambitious installations, and more performance-based work.

Tate St Ives opened in 1993 to exhibit works by the artists who had lived and worked in the area. The nearby Barbara Hepworth Museum and Sculpture Garden had been placed in the care of Tate since 1980.

In 1992 the Tate trustees decided to open a second London gallery for international modern and contemporary art. The site was the former Bankside Power Station designed by Sir Giles Gilbert Scott. Built in two phases between 1947 and 1963, the power station had fallen into disuse due to rising oil prices. Swiss architects Herzog & de Meuron preserved much of the original structure, including the vast expanse of the Turbine Hall, while constructing a glass-panelled light box on the roof that allows natural light to seep down into the building.

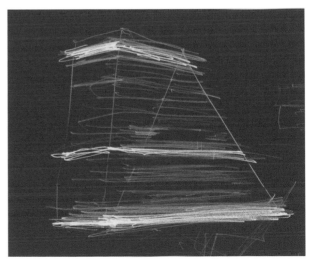
Early sketch of the new building by Herzog & de Meuron

TURBINE HALL

Originally housing the electricity generators in Bankside Power Station, the Turbine Hall is a vast public space.

Since 2000, it has become one of the gallery's most distinctive features, providing the setting for some of the most spectacular and talked-about artworks of the twenty-first century.

Initially sponsored by Unilever, a range of international artists have created a series of specially commissioned works for the Turbine Hall. Louise Bourgeois constructed the towers *I Do, I Undo, I Redo*, and placed the twelve-metre high spider *Maman* on the bridge. Anish Kapoor filled the whole length of the space with *Marsyas*. With Olafur Eliasson's *The Weather Project*, the sun seemed to peer down through a hazy mist. *Test Site* by Carsten Höller installed five giant slides. Doris Salcedo broke open a crevice in the floor of the museum with *Shibboleth* and Ai Weiwei installed a sea of porcelain *Sunflower Seeds*.

A new series of Turbine Hall commissions, sponsored by Hyundai Motor, began in 2015 with Abraham Cruzvillegas's *Empty Lot*, followed in 2016 by Philippe Parreno. With a new bridge on level 4, linking the Boiler House and the Switch House, the Turbine Hall remains at the heart of Tate Modern.

Olafur Eliasson
The Weather Project (The Unilever Series) 2003

BOILER HOUSE

The Boiler House includes one floor for ticketed exhibitions, and two floors of free displays of work from the Tate collection, entitled *Four Approaches to Modern Art (1900 to Now)*.

Each of the free displays looks at a distinct aspect of modern and contemporary art, bringing together a wide variety of works from different periods and different parts of the world.

Level 2 includes the Start Display, an introductory space that has been designed particularly for the first-time visitor. *In the Studio* focuses on the often intensely personal experience of making and looking at art, and *Artist and Society* shows artworks that address broader social and political issues.

On level 4, *Media Networks* examines the ways in which artists have responded to developments in media and communications technology, while *Materials and Objects* highlights the extraordinary range of materials and techniques used by artists over the last hundred years.

View of level 4, *Media Networks* display

START DISPLAY

The Start Display is an introductory space, intended for people visiting a museum of modern art for the first time.

Presenting a selection of major works from the Tate collection, it encourages different ways of looking at art, and suggests helpful questions that you can ask yourself as you are walking around the rest of the museum.

The choice of works in the Start Display is likely to change from year to year. In the first year, they were chosen around the theme of colour. Including examples of painting, sculpture, collage and conceptual art by artists such as Alexander Calder, Wassily Kandinsky and Ellsworth Kelly, the display explores how we perceive colour, the connections between colour and memory, and the emotional or spiritual values that we assign to different colours.

Benode Behari Mukherjee
Lady with Fruit 1957

Known as a painter and a pioneer of modern art in India, Mukherjee lost his sight when he was in his fifties. Undeterred, he began to explore new ways of making art, including paper cut-outs. At his direction, his assistants cut simple shapes from coloured paper, which Mukherjee arranged into complex compositions. For Mukherjee, colour possessed symbolic and spiritual values. He worked by memory and intuition, feeling that he could sense the colour of the paper by touch.

Henri Matisse
The Snail 1953

Like Mukherjee, Matisse began to make cut-outs when he was too ill to make paintings. Often confined to his bed or a wheelchair, he would cut shapes from sheets of paper painted in bright colours, which were positioned on the wall according to his instructions. 'The contour of the figure springs from the discovery of the scissors that give it the movement of circulating life', he explained. Here the rotating paper shapes radiate out in a spiral, echoing a snail's shell, to form what Matisse described as 'abstraction rooted in reality'.

IN THE STUDIO

In the Studio is about the close engagement of the individual with a work of art, whether making art or looking at art.

The image of an artist in his or her studio suggests that they have shut themselves off from the world to allow a period of intensive concentration. Of course, artists work in different ways, and in many different environments. An artwork can be made in a foundry, in a darkroom, or in the middle of a field. Nor does it have to be a solitary act. Some works based on performance or social interaction could involve hundreds of participants. Yet there are artists whose work is profoundly inward-looking, who depict the details of their domestic lives, or even – like some of the surrealists – explore their own subconscious as a source of images.

Just as making a work of art requires concentrated engagement, so too can the act of looking at one. Mark Rothko's Seagram murals were famously donated to Tate because the artist felt that the restaurant for which they were originally intended would not be a suitable setting for them. He wanted his paintings to be seen in an enclosed space that would encourage a more immersive and contemplative experience.

Art can also make us aware of the complexity of seeing, emphasising the psychological or philosophical influences on our perception, whether using optical effects that dazzle and disrupt our vision, or introducing distorted forms that seem to convey a profound sense of unease.

Edgar Degas
Little Dancer aged Fourteen 1880–1,
cast c.1922

This sculpture of a young ballerina was originally made from wax. It was dressed in a real silk bodice, a gauze tutu and ballet shoes, with a wig that was probably made of horsehair. Degas applied a coloured tint to make the flesh more life-like. When it was exhibited in Paris in 1881, visitors were shocked at the unprecedented realism of the figure. After Degas's death, a series of bronze casts were made. In keeping with the artist's vision, they were again dressed with a gauze tutu, while a real ribbon was tied around the cast bronze hair.

Georges Braque
Mandora 1909–10

Braque painted several still lifes featuring musical instruments during the winter of 1909–10. This was part of the critical period when he and Pablo Picasso worked closely together, establishing a technique of painting known as cubism that could suggest a series of shifting perspectives. A mandora is a small instrument similar to a lute, and the fragmented surface of the painting has its own musical quality, creating a shimmering sense of movement and rhythm.

Salvador Dalí
Metamorphosis of Narcissus 1937

Dalí was fascinated by double images and curious resemblances between apparently different objects. In this painting the doubling represents a magical moment of transformation. The kneeling figure on the left is Narcissus, a character in Greek mythology who fell in love with his own reflection and pined away. After his death, the gods immortalised him as a flower, which sprouts out of the egg clutched between the raised fingers on the right.

Leonor Fini
Little Hermit Sphinx 1948

Fini's image of the Sphinx (a mythological hybrid of a lion and woman) can be seen partly as a self-portrait. She regarded the Sphinx as a symbolic intermediary between the human and animal realms, and between the conscious mind and the deeper recesses of the imagination. Her position, crouched in the doorway of a decrepit building, similarly suggests a threshold between different states of being. A human lung is suspended from a lintel, while she toys with the scattered bones of a bird.

René Magritte
The Annunciation 1930

The objects in this painting appear to be a metal sheet with bells, a paper cut-out and two balusters. These innocuous decorative items have been enlarged to loom as vast, forbidding monuments in a mysterious rocky landscape. The title *The Annunciation* traditionally refers to the angel Gabriel's visit to the Virgin Mary, and may have been intended by Magritte as a joke against religion. But it may also suggest that something momentous is about to happen in this eerie setting.

Alberto Giacometti
Diego 1959

Giacometti frequently used his brother Diego as a model. The artist regarded each sitting as a new experience, stating 'When he poses for me I don't recognise him'. Nonetheless, his observations deepened over the years and were condensed into images of great intensity, especially in the late 1950s. The dark background of this work places greater visual emphasis on the head, which is sombre, isolated and perhaps apprehensive.

Shafic Abboud
Composition c.1957–8

In the 1950s Abboud often worked by laying paint thickly onto the canvas, applying and shaping it with a palette knife to create an intense sense of movement. He was born in Lebanon, but spent most of his life in Paris, where this work was made. The blues and greys in this abstract painting seem to carry memories of the light and colour of his homeland.

Ibrahim El-Salahi
Reborn Sounds of Childhood Dreams I 1961–5

El-Salahi studied painting in Khartoum in the late 1940s, before completing his studies in London. Returning to Khartoum in 1957, he realised that Sudan – a newly independent country in the midst of a civil war – required a different approach in his art. As one of the founders of the Khartoum School, he developed a new visual vocabulary comprising simple forms, strong lines and sombre colours inspired by his environment and rooted in Arabic and African art and writing.

Lee Krasner
Gothic Landscape 1961

Although this is an abstract painting,
the thick vertical lines that dominate
its centre can be seen as trees, with
thick knotted roots at their base. It was
probably this that led Krasner to call the
painting *Gothic Landscape*, several years
after completing it. *Gothic Landscape*
was made in the years following the
death of her husband Jackson Pollock
from a car crash in 1956. It belongs to
a series of large canvases whose violent
and expressive gestural brushstrokes
reflected her feelings of grief.

Mark Rothko
Black on Maroon 1958

In the late 1950s, Rothko was commissioned to paint a series of murals for the fashionable Four Seasons restaurant, in the Seagram Building on Park Avenue, New York. As he worked, however, the murals assumed a more sober character, dominated by maroon, dark red and black. Recognising that a high-end restaurant was not the ideal location for such a work, Rothko withdrew from the commission and finally presented the series to the Iate Gallery. Presented as the artist intended, in reduced light and in a compact space, the subtlety of the layered surfaces slowly emerges, revealing their solemn and meditative character.

ARTIST
AND SOCIETY

This display looks at some of the ways in which artists engage with the world around them. In the first half of the twentieth century, some artists believed that there was an implicit parallel between the development of a new visual language in modern art and the promise of a new society.

The clean lines and balanced compositions of abstract painting and sculpture seemed to correspond to the utopian ideals of the time. Then, as the world descended into brutality and war, artists felt impelled to bear witness to the horrors and remember the victims.

Art can also provide a powerful means of protesting against social injustice or drawing attention to those who have campaigned to change the world. Sometimes directly and sometimes more obliquely, artists have commemorated the heroes of the battle against apartheid in South Africa, the civil rights struggle in the United States, and the women's rights movement in India. Just as profoundly, artists have documented the experience of everyday life, and the day-to-day struggles of ordinary people around the world.

Lucia Moholy
Bauhaus Building, Dessau, view from the vestibule window looking toward the workshop wing 1926

Lucia Moholy moved to Dessau to accompany her husband László Moholy-Nagy when he began teaching at the Bauhaus school of art, architecture and design. Established by the architect Walter Gropius, the Bauhaus was associated with a utopian vision that would integrate arts and crafts with everyday life. Composed with a determinedly modernist eye, Moholy's photographs document the architecture of the buildings.

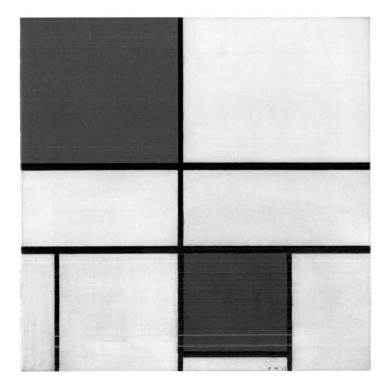

Piet Mondrian
Composition C (No.III) with Red, Yellow and Blue 1935

Mondrian developed a geometric form of abstract art that, in its purest form, used only the primary colours, black and white, and grids of straight lines. He was influenced by the mysticism of Theosophy, which claimed there was a universal order beyond the world of natural appearances. In his paintings Mondrian hoped to evoke this sense of equilibrium, with all the elements in a balanced, though never symmetrical, relationship.

Pablo Picasso
Weeping Woman 1937

In 1937, as a response to the Spanish Civil War, Picasso produced over forty images of a woman engulfed in tears. The figure originated in his mural *Guernica*, which depicted the devastating aerial bombardment of the small Basque town. *Weeping Woman* is the culmination of the series. The features of the woman were modelled on Picasso's then-partner Dora Maar, making this an intensely personal image as well as an emblem of the suffering of the Spanish nation.

Malangatana Ngwenya
Untitled 1967

During the 1960s Malangatana took part in the struggle for independence in Mozambique. He was arrested by the Portuguese secret police and imprisoned for eighteen months. This work depicts the chaos and suffering of a society at war with itself. The figures overlap, seeming to merge into one another, filling the frame so that we have no sense of context or perspective. Instead the image is dominated by white gnashing teeth, claw-like hands and the wide eyes of humans and animals.

Theaster Gates
Civil Tapestry 4 2011

In May 1963, a group of black school children and students were marching peacefully for equal rights in Birmingham, Alabama. Police used powerful fire hoses to break up the march, injuring many of the young protestors. Gates has arranged strips of decommissioned fire hoses to resemble the composition of a 1960s American abstract painting – a form that pointedly failed to engage with the Civil Rights movement. Gates also questions whether the protestors' goals have been fulfilled. 'Some of us are slightly better while others are a great deal better', he has reflected, 'but… things are far from equal'.

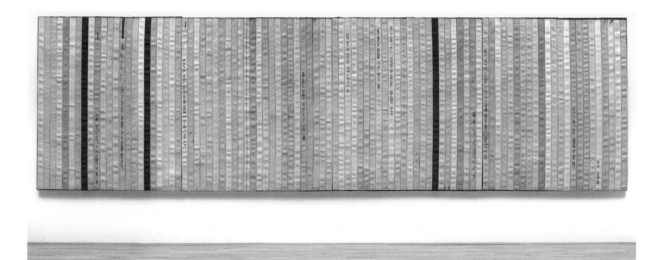

Sue Williamson
Lilian Ngoyi from *A Few South Africans* 1983

Williamson was closely involved in the struggle against apartheid in South Africa. This series of prints celebrates the often unsung role played by women in the campaign, with accompanying texts by the artist. Each print combines a number of techniques on paper, bringing together elements that relate to the sitter's biography. The decorative border surrounding each portrait pays homage to the custom in the South African townships of displaying important photographs with coloured papers and other printed materials.

Richard Hamilton
The citizen 1981–3

The citizen was based on stills from a 1980 news report about the IRA 'dirty protest'. After the government revoked their Special Category status and began to treat them as ordinary criminals, inmates in Long Kesh decided to wear only prison blankets and to daub their cell walls with excrement. Hamilton wrote that he could not 'condone the methods' of the IRA, but was struck by the resemblance to images of Christian martyrdom.

MEDIA NETWORKS

This display explores some of the different ways in which artists have responded to the impact of mass media and communications, reflecting on a world increasingly shaped by advertising, television and digital technology.

The rapid pace of industrialisation, the unprecedented growth of cities, the speed of modern transportation, the cult of the machine, and revolutionary developments in communications technology all had an impact on the art of the early twentieth century. New approaches to painting and sculpture attempted to capture that swirling sense of energy and excitement.

In the 1950s and 1960s the colourful imagery associated with comic books, advertising and Hollywood cinema had a similar impact, providing inspiration for pop art. Yet artists around the world approached such images in different ways. While many British and American artists seemed to wryly celebrate consumerism and the cult of celebrity, artists in Eastern Europe and Latin America were more directly subversive, and feminist artists challenged the gender stereotypes prevalent in the mass media.

Today, artists continue to engage with the new visual culture that is emerging from digital technology. Their responses can range from creating works that exist on internet platforms to exploring the instantaneous imagery of social media.

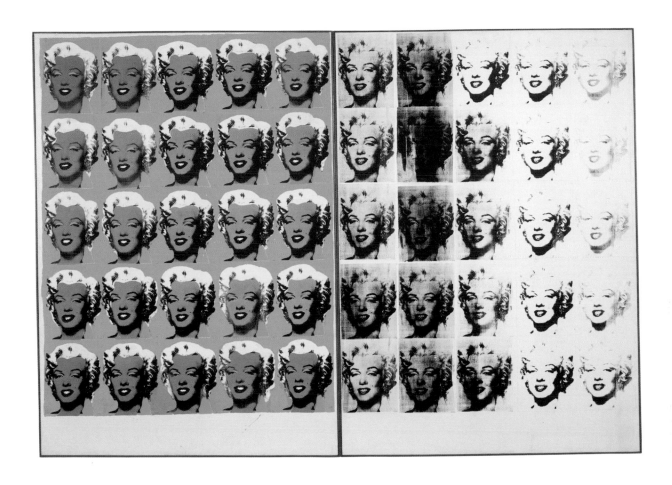

Andy Warhol
Marilyn Diptych 1962

Marilyn Monroe died in August 1962. Over the next few months, Warhol made more than twenty silkscreen paintings of her, all based on the same publicity photograph from the 1953 film *Niagara*. Here the repetition of her image seems to intensify its powerful presence, so that it comes to resemble a religion icon. The way the images in the right panel seems to fade away suggests the star's tragic decline.

Sonia Delaunay
Triptych 1963

Sonia Delaunay was a pioneer of abstract painting, whose work extended beyond fine art into fashion, textiles, costume and set design, interior decoration, architecture and advertising. She and her artist husband Robert Delaunay developed a distinctive approach to abstraction called simultanism, exploring how our perception of colours changes when they are placed alongside each other. This work was made when she was in her late seventies. She called it *Triptych* because it brings together three different motifs that she had been working on.

Umberto Boccioni
Unique Forms of Continuity in Space 1913, cast 1972

Boccioni was closely associated with futurism, an early twentieth-century movement that provocatively called for artists to reject old-fashioned ideas of beauty and celebrate the achievements of the machine age. The futurists were especially concerned with depicting motion. This is one of a series of striding sculptures, in which Boccioni represented movement as a continuous flowing form, like a blurred photograph, so that his figures seem to exist simultaneously at different moments in time.

Fernand Léger
Still Life with a Beer Mug 1921–2

While serving in the First World War, Léger became convinced that art should be accessible to ordinary working people. He moved away from the pure abstraction of his earlier work towards the stylised depiction of real objects. This painting shows a workman's lunch on a table. However, the colourful patterns on the mug contrast with the decorative surfaces on the floor and in the background to create a complex composition that dazzles the eye.

Max Beckmann
Carnival 1920

This work represents the climax of Carnival, a season of fancy dress parties, masked balls and street processions with wild music and dancing. The two figures are based on close friends of the artist, who is possibly represented by the masked clown. With its grotesque and distorted figures, Beckmann's work epitomised what the Nazis considered to be 'degenerate' art. He was dismissed from his teaching post in Frankfurt in 1933. Several of his works were included in the 1937 *Degenerate Art* show, prompting him to leave Germany.

Roy Lichtenstein
Whaam! 1963

In the 1960s, Lichtenstein made a series of paintings based on sources such as comic books, advertisements and mail-order catalogues. Recasting these small, mass-produced images as large-scale canvases, he would adjust the composition for greater dramatic effect, while still carefully imitating the appearance of the original printed materials. He was particularly drawn to war and romance comics, presenting their highly emotional subject matter in a detached, impersonal manner.

Guerrilla Girls
Do Women Have To Be Naked To Get Into the Met. Museum? 1989

The Guerrilla Girls are an anonymous activist group who highlight discrimination in the art world. Initially focusing on sexism, they have also addressed racism and other areas of social and gender-based inequality. For public appearances and interviews they hide their identities beneath gorilla masks. Parodying a painting by the nineteenth-century French artist Jean-Auguste-Dominique Ingres, this poster first appeared as an advertisement on New York City buses, paid for by the Guerrilla Girls themselves, until the bus company cancelled their leasing agreement on grounds of indecency.

Barbara Kruger
Who owns what? 2012

Barbara Kruger's images grab the viewer's attention with an approach that is instantly recognisable, using found photographs that are cropped, manipulated and printed in black and white, and overlaid with text enclosed in a block of red. Directly addressing the viewer, her words challenge us to think about gender politics and the culture of consumerism. The three simple words in *Who owns what?* can be placed into many different contexts, confronting the viewer with the numerous social faultlines created by inequality.

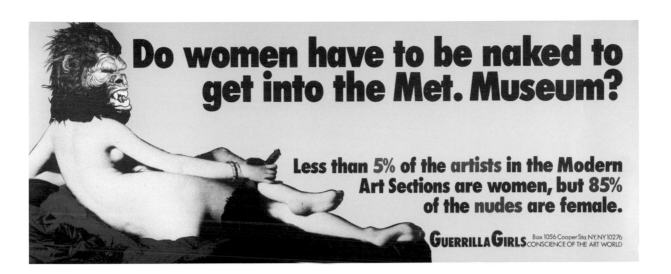

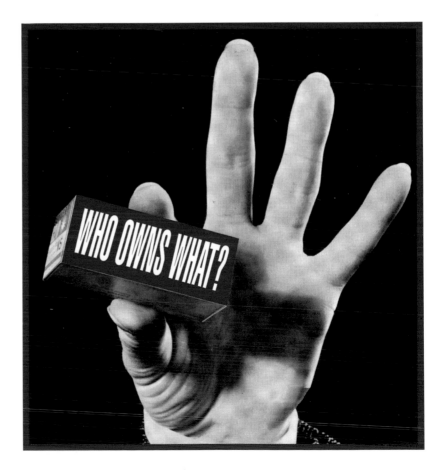

Cildo Meireles
Babel 2001

Meireles refers to *Babel* as a 'tower of incomprehension'. Stacked with hundreds of radios, each tuned to a different station and adjusted to the minimum volume at which it is audible, the sculpture relates to the biblical story of the Tower of Babel, a tower tall enough to reach the heavens. God was affronted by this structure, and caused the builders to speak in different languages, so they become divided and scattered across the earth.

Nam June Paik
Bakelite Robot 2002

This sculptural figure was constructed using nine vintage Bakelite radios, which Paik acquired from thrift stores and markets. Bakelite was an early heat-resistant plastic that was commonly used for domestic electrical goods and children's toys. Paik has customised the radios to incorporate specially compiled video footage. Their archaic quality harks back to an era when global communications technology was just beginning to become part of everyday life.

MATERIALS
AND OBJECTS

Traditionally, certain materials have been associated with fine art in western Europe, whether applying oil paint to canvas, printing ink onto paper, or making sculpture from bronze, stone or wood. Over the last hundred years or so, however, artists have embraced a proliferation of alternative possibilities.

In the early years of the twentieth century artists such as Pablo Picasso and Georges Braque began to use collage, combining paint with disparate materials such as newspapers, wallpaper patterns and advertisements. The principle of introducing elements from the real world was taken a step further by Marcel Duchamp's idea of the 'readymade' – an ordinary manufactured object that has been selected by the artist and designated as a work of art. By the 1960s the artist Louise Nevelson was creating sculptures composed of discarded or broken items that she found on the streets of New York City.

A different approach can be seen in the work of the Japanese mono-ha group. Rather than shaping or carving materials to impose their own vision on them, they wanted to open the viewer's eyes to the inherent qualities of the materials, and encouraged people to reflect on their relationship to their surroundings and to the natural world.

For today's artists, organic materials can be intertwined with mass-produced industrial products. There is a similar freedom in the techniques that are employed, whether using traditional craft techniques or impersonal manufacturing methods.

El Anatsui
Ink Splash II 2012

From a distance, El Anatsui's *Ink Splash II* appears to be a mess of blue spilt over a shimmering metallic surface. Looking closer, you can see that the artist has created the whole work using flattened bottle tops which he has painstakingly woven together with copper wire. Recycling discarded objects from Nigeria, where he lives, El Anatsui gives them new purpose in a response to European and American traditions of abstract painting.

Marcel Duchamp
Fountain 1917, replica 1964

Fountain is the most famous of Marcel Duchamp's so-called 'readymades' – an ordinary manufactured object that has been designated by the artist as a work of art. It was purchased from a sanitary ware supplier and submitted under the pseudonym Richard Mutt to the newly established Society of Independent Artists in New York, which had pledged to promote and exhibit all varieties of modern art. As Duchamp may have anticipated, the Society rejected it, prompting a heated argument about whether it was a work of art or not.

Koshimizu Susumu
From Surface to Surface 1971,
remade 1976

From Surface to Surface investigates the
substance of wood by sawing planks into
different shapes, exposing their surface
qualities through different kinds of
repetitive cuts. In the late 1960s and early
1970s Koshimizu was associated with a
group of Tokyo artists known as mono-ha,
usually translated as the 'school of things'.
Their work emphasised an attention to
materials and explored the relationship
between a sculpture and the surrounding
space to make the viewer more aware
of 'the world as it is'.

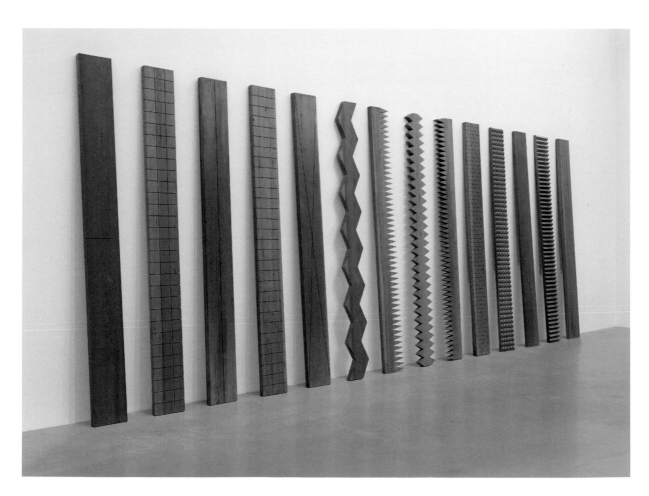

Lee Ufan
Relatum 1968, 1994

Lee Ufan's sculptural works focus on the essential character and presence of their materials and their interconnections. Here he uses a single material – one hundred flat bands of stainless steel – and explores how the different elements relate to one another and to the space in which they are arranged. 'A work of art, rather than being a self-complete, independent entity, is a resonant relationship with the outside', he has said. 'It exists together with the world, simultaneously what it is and what it is not.'

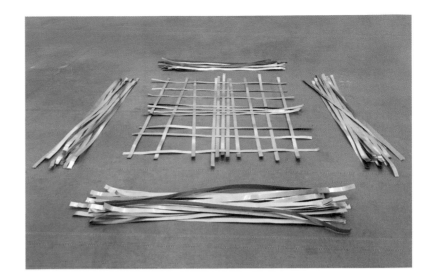

Magdalena Abakanowicz
Embryology 1978–80

Polish sculptor Magdalena Abakanowicz began making these cocoon-like objects in the 1970s. She sewed together burlap sacking, nylon stockings, rags and rope to create hundreds of soft sculptures of varying shapes and sizes, 'rounded like bellies, or elongated like mummies,' as she described them. Made at a time of political tension between the Soviet Union and Poland, the work 'could be understood as a cry from behind the Iron Curtain', Abakanowicz has said.

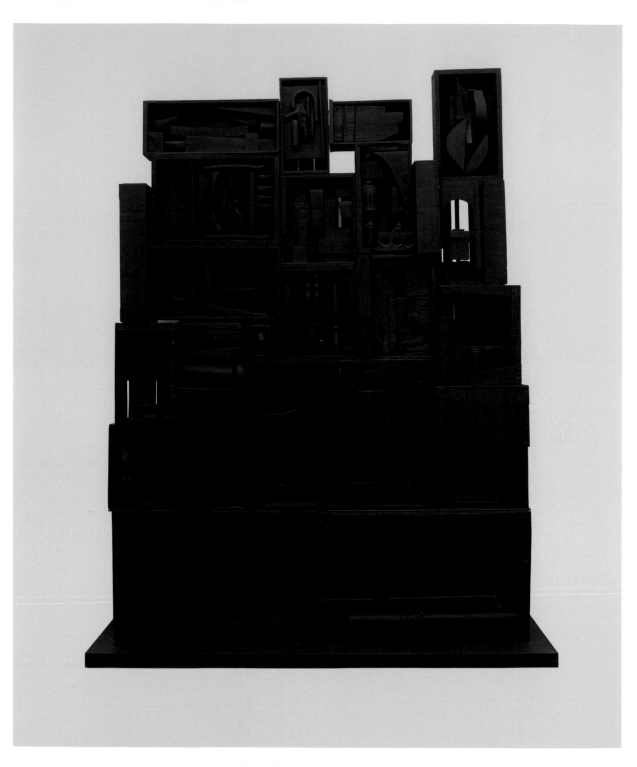

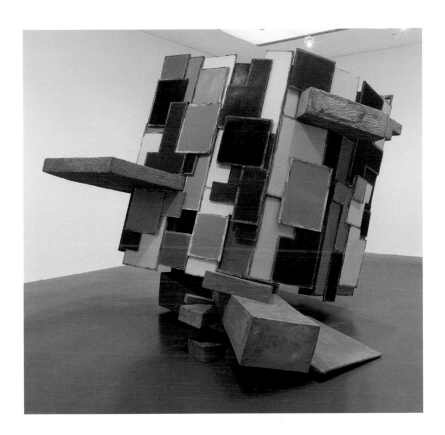

Louise Nevelson
Black Wall 1959

In the late 1950s, Nevelson began to make reliefs by stacking wooden boxes and crates, each of which would contain an arrangement of found objects that she collected as she walked around the streets of New York City. *Black Wall* is an early example of this approach, filled with pieces of scrap timber, such as joinery offcuts and fragments of furniture. The disparate elements are unified by being painted black, a colour which Nevelson suggested will make any material look more distinguished.

Phyllida Barlow
untitled: upturnedhouse, 2 2012

Phyllida Barlow uses everyday household or DIY materials which she transforms through processes of layering or accumulation to make large-scale sculptural installations. This work is made of painted wood panels that are built up to form an irregular structure. The materials can be deceptive, as the two wedge-shaped elements that support the structure appear to be concrete, but are in fact made of wood with a surface coating of cement. The construction looks ready to collapse at any moment, flagrantly disobeying the rules of balance, symmetry, gravity and beauty associated with more classical forms of sculpture and architecture.

Niki de Saint Phalle
Shooting Picture 1961

Saint Phalle's *Shooting Pictures* were
created by concealing small bags of liquid
paint beneath layers of plaster mounted
on blockboard. The artist or her friends
fired a gun at this pure white surface, so
that colour burst out and streamed down
the front of the painting. Saint Phalle gave
up the series after feeling that she had
become addicted to shooting, 'like one
becomes addicted to a drug'.

Shimamoto Shozo
Holes 1954

Holes was made from layers of pasted
newspapers. The surface was painted
white with hints of pale blue, then pierced
to reveal the different layers underneath.
Shimamoto began the series around 1949
or 1950, during the postwar American
occupation of Japan. The contrast
between delicacy and violence may reflect
the fracturing of traditional Japanese
culture in the wake of the Second World
War. This balance between destructive
and creative action was a key element
in the work of the Gutai Art Association
(1954–72), of which Shimamoto was
a founder.

SWITCH HOUSE

The Switch House is a new extension to Tate Modern, which was completed in 2016.

Rising to ten floors, the variety of new spaces include Tate Exchange, a dedicated centre for learning and engagement, and a viewing platform offering remarkable views across the city. A new entrance to the south means that the museum now represents a link between the north and south of the city.

The new displays, entitled *How Art Became Active (1960 to Now)*, focus on developments over the last fifty or so years. Rather than regarding the artwork as a self-contained object, artists are thinking more dynamically about its relationship to the viewer, to the physical space around it, and its relationship to society.

At the base of the building are the Tanks, a space designed with live art, performance and expanded cinema in mind. Above that, the displays on level 2 examine the relation between art and architecture, level 3 looks at works that bring art closer to everyday life, while level 4 includes *Living Cities* and galleries dedicated to the ARTIST ROOMS programme – with a display that changes every year, looking in depth at a single artist.

Switch House: Level 10, Viewing Level (visualisation)

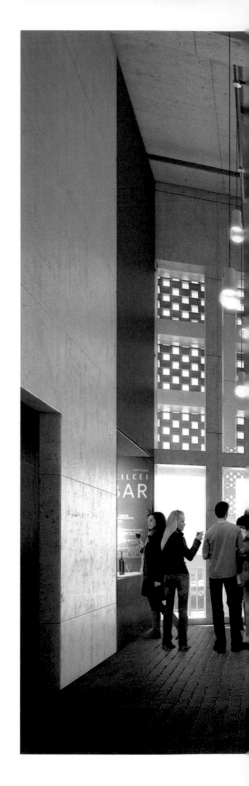

THE TANKS

Converted from the former oil tanks of Bankside Power Station, these cavernous spaces form the foundation of the Switch House.

Retaining their raw, industrial character, the Tanks are designed to showcase live art, installation, and the moving image. In recent decades, artists have increasingly engaged with areas such as performance, expanded cinema, broadcast media, social activism, or works that explore the relationship between artist and audience. The Tanks provide an opportunity to look at the history of these developments as well as current practice.

Switch House: Level 0, East Tank (visualisation)

BETWEEN OBJECT AND ARCHITECTURE

The artists in this display explore the relationship between the work of art and the space around it, and what this implies for the viewer who is also part of that spatial environment.

In some cases artists use materials associated with the city, such as bricks, concrete and glass, which create a dialogue between the sculpture and the surrounding architecture. Works made with steel and aluminium echo modern industrial features such as ducts and piping.

The display includes photographs that underline the relationship between geometric abstraction and the urban landscape. There are sculptures that explore forms such as cubes or rectangular solids, implying a relationship between the artwork and the dimensions of the room in which it is displayed. Others are designed to occupy corners and doorways, hang from the ceiling, or climb the wall of the gallery.

Many of these works encourage us to think about our behaviour in relation to them. We do not just look at them, we walk around them and peer into them, sometimes walk through them or over them.

Lygia Clark
Creature-Maquette (320) 1964

Brazilian artist Lygia Clark made a series of geometric, hinged-aluminium sculptures which she titled *Creatures* ('Bichos' in Portuguese), for which this is a working model. She compared the hinges to the intersecting bones of an animal skeleton. The sculptures were originally intended to be manipulated by hand, and could take many possible forms. Clark believed that the viewer's active participation was essential for the work.

Saloua Raouda Choucair
Infinite Structure 1963–5

Choucair's painting and sculpture combines European abstraction with Arab and Islamic traditions. Many of her sculptures are composed of interlocking pieces, which build to create a larger structure resembling a column or a wall. Choucair has compared these pieces to the stanzas of Islamic and Sufi poetry, each with its own rhythm and meaning while also forming part of a greater whole. *Infinite Structure*, a tower of multiple rectangular stone blocks, also reflects her affinity with architectural structures. Choucair once said that given another life to live she would choose to be an architect.

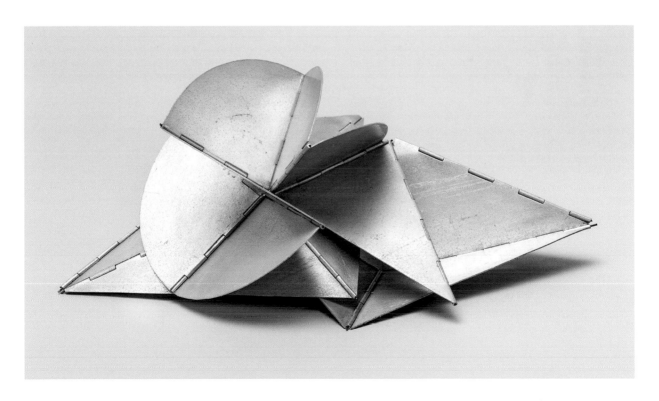

Mary Martin
Inversions 1966

Martin was interested in the relationship
between art and architecture, and made
a number of reliefs for public spaces.
She was mindful of the relationship
between the object and the wall behind
it, but also the questions of proportion
and variation involved in designing large
structures. The ninety-six reflective
aluminium panels in this work mirror their
surroundings and the passing viewers.
They have been angled according to a
sequence of permutations, which are then
repeated backwards as the 'inversions'
of the title.

Cristina Iglesias
Pavilion Suspended in a Room I 2005

Viewers are invited to enter and explore this open-ended space, defined by a sequence of latticework panels. The decorative designs on the screens seem to evoke Moorish abstract art but, on closer inspection, letters and words can be discerned. These comprise an extract from Arthur C. Clarke's science-fiction novel *Rendezvous with Rama* (1973) which describes the discovery of a vast spacecraft that contains an extraordinary architectural landscape.

Roni Horn
Pink Tons 2009

As an artist, Horn is fascinated by
ambiguity and processes of change.
A large glass sculpture, *Pink Tons* is
an imposingly solid presence in the
gallery. Yet its appearance is continually
changing, as the natural light that passes
through it varies in intensity at different
times of day. Looking onto the top surface
of the sculpture, the sense of heaviness
gives way to an impression of liquidity,
like staring into a body of clear water.

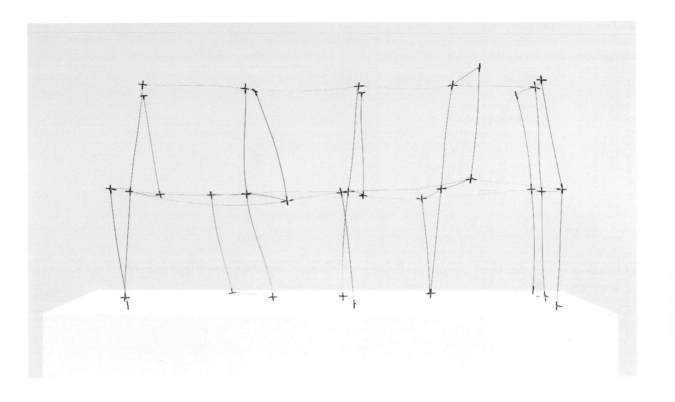

Gego
Horizontal Square Reticularia 71/10 1971

The Venezuelan artist Gertrude Goldschmidt worked under the name Gego. Many of her sculptures seem to refer to a tradition in modern art of using grids and geometric lines. At first glance, this structure seems to be composed of a series of squares. However, the thin steel rods and metal joints that hold it together have a tendency to bend and waver, while some of the connecting lines are missing. This interplay between solid geometric and flexible organic forms is essential to Gego's work.

PERFORMER AND PARTICIPANT

This display features artists who – in different ways – have wanted to break down the boundaries between art and real life.

Several of the works are based on performances, which can involve generating a direct moment of communication or confrontation between the artist and the audience. These are represented on film, in photographs or through sculptural props that imply certain actions and movements.

There are also works that emerge from an artist's engagement with a particular community or social group, such as conducting research into social conditions or recording people's memories. In other works, collective actions emerge from traditional crafts or practices.

The display also includes installations that invite the viewer's active participation, with environments to walk through, spaces to explore and interactive elements, so that the work becomes something to be experienced rather than merely looked at.

Ana Lupas
The Solemn Process (1964–74/76; 1980–5; 1985–2008)

In the 1960s, Romanian artist Ana Lupas worked with villagers in Transylvania to create large structures inspired by the local tradition of weaving wreaths for harvest festivals. Made using natural materials such as straw, hemp, cotton, clay and wood, the individual objects would decay, but the process of making them continued from year to year. Over time, however, as traditional skills declined, Lupas found that fewer participants were able to take part in her project. Concerned to preserve the structures, she sealed them into metal casings – a solution that balanced the natural and traditional with modern, industrial techniques.

Meschac Gaba
Architecture Room from *Museum of Contemporary African Art* 1997–2002

Benin artist Meschac Gaba conceived his *Museum of Contemporary African Art* during a residency in Amsterdam. As he explored museums in Europe for the first time, he realised that these existing institutions would not be able to accommodate the kind of art that he wanted to create. 'I needed a space for my work, because this did not exist', he has said. Over the next few years, he developed a series of rooms, creating spaces devoted to architecture, religion, money, games and other aspects of everyday life, where visitors would not merely look at objects but engage in social activities, study and play.

Marina Abramovic
Rhythm 0 1974

Serbian performance artist Marina Abramovic staged this work at a gallery in Naples in 1974. Seventy-two objects were set out on a table, including a gun, a knife and an axe, a feather, paint, shoes, bread, a candle and a spoon. For six hours she allowed members of the public to pick up these items and use them on her in any way they wished. Here the objects are similarly laid out on a table, while a slide projection shows what happened during the performance.

LIVING
CITIES

The George Economou Gallery

This display looks at a variety of responses to the modern
city, with artists from around the world exploring the
urban landscape.

The perspectives range from panoramic overviews that
attempt to map the whole city to close-up photographs
recording the minutiae of daily life.

Above all the city is seen as a fluid space that is always
changing. Works deal with patterns of migration, and the
different communities that emerge and adapt. The use
of surprising materials such as rubber or couscous,
or a focus on colours, encourages us to look at the city
in imaginative new ways.

Boris Mikhailov
Red 1968–75, printed c.1999–2000
(detail)

Since the late 1960s, Mikhailov has photographed his home city of Kharkov in Ukraine. Often arranged into complex installations, his work goes beyond simple documentation to analyse the effects of social and political conditions. All of the images in this series contain something red. This colour, symbolising communism, is a reminder of the inescapable presence of the Soviet regime, and how its ideology permeated every aspect of daily life.

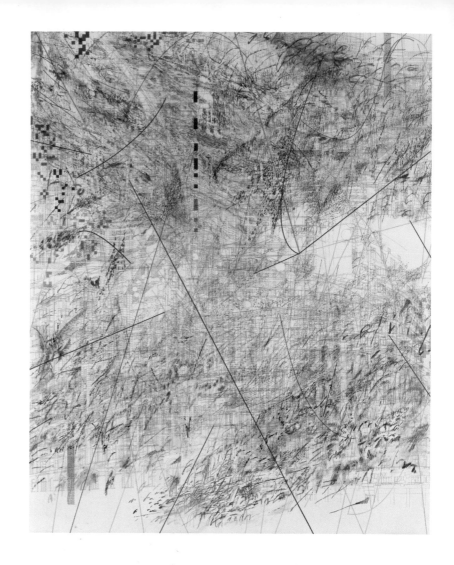

Julie Mehretu
*Mogamma, A Painting in Four Parts:
Part 3* 2012

Mehretu's painting takes its name from
a government building in Tahrir Square
in Cairo. As a symbol of the Egyptian
government it provided a focus for the
2011 protests against Hosni Mubarak's
authoritarian regime. The painting is
covered with overlapping architectural
drawings of the Mogamma and other
locations related to popular protest,
such as Meskel Square in Addis Ababa
and Zuccotti Park in New York, the site
of the 'Occupy' camp. On top of this,
Mehretu has added a dense surface
of marks and brushstrokes.

Marwan Rechmaoui
Beirut Caoutchouc 2004–8

Beirut Caoutchouc is a large floor-based rubber map of the city of Beirut. Embossed in precise detail with roads and highways, and segmented into sixty individual pieces demarcating neighbourhoods in the city, Rechmaoui's installation examines the physical and social formation of one of the world's most conflicted cities. By inviting people to walk over the piece, it also demands that viewers should engage with the city as individuals.

ARTIST ROOMS

A series of rooms on level 4 of the Switch House are devoted to showing work from ARTIST ROOMS, a collection of work that is jointly owned and managed by National Galleries of Scotland and Tate on behalf of the nation.

Founded in 2008 by Anthony d'Offay, the collection gathers major groups of artworks by leading contemporary artists, so that whole rooms or exhibitions of their work can be made available to museums and galleries throughout the UK. The collection now includes more than 1,600 works. The programme has a special emphasis on engaging young people with contemporary art.

The ARTIST ROOMS galleries at Tate Modern will host a series of year-long exhibitions, beginning with Louise Bourgeois.

Louise Bourgeois
Spider 1994

TATE BRITAIN
TATE LIVERPOOL
TATE ST IVES

Tate Britain is the home of British art from 1500 to the present day, including the world's largest collection of work by J.M.W. Turner. The free displays present a chronological walk through the history of British art, with Spotlight rooms focusing on particular themes. As well as a stimulating exhibition programme, the gallery presents a major artistic commission in the Duveen galleries each year, and regularly hosts the Turner Prize.

Tate Liverpool is dedicated to international modern and contemporary art. Opening in 1988, the building was converted from a former warehouse on the Albert Dock, once a key hub for international trade. With an active education programme, the gallery encourages a new younger, audience. Major exhibitions have included surveys of work by Jackson Pollock, Andy Warhol, Francis Bacon, Sarah Lucas, Gustav Klimt and Piet Mondrian.

Tate St Ives is located on the coast of Cornwall, in a town whose unique landscape and quality of light have attracted artists since Victorian times. Overlooking Porthmeor Beach and facing out to the Atlantic Ocean, the gallery celebrates the remarkable variety of artists who lived or worked in the area, including Alfred Wallis, Ben Nicholson, Naum Gabo and Barbara Hepworth, whose former studio is now a Museum and Sculpture Garden managed by Tate.

CREDITS

Meireles: Purchased jointly by Tate, London (with the assistance of the Latin American Acquisitions Committee) and the D.Daskalopoulos Collection, 2013, as a promised gift to Tate. © Cildo Meireles. Courtesy Galerie Lelong, New York

Mikhailov: Purchased with assistance from the Art Fund (with a contribution from the Wolfson Foundation) and Konstantin Grigorishin 2011. © Boris Mikhailov

Moholy: Purchased 2011. © Hattula Moholy-Nagy/DACS 2016

Mondrian: Lent from a private collection 1981. ©2016 Mondrian/Holtzman Trust

Mukherjee: Purchased with funds provided by the South Asia Acquisitions Committee 2015. © Estate of the artist

Nevelson: Presented by the Friends of the Tate Gallery 1962. © ARS, NY and DACS, London 2016

Ngwenya: Purchased with funds provided by the Africa Acquisitions Committee 2014. © Estate of Malangatana Ngwenya

Paik: Purchased with funds provided by Hyundai, Asia Pacific Acquisitions Committee and Tate Americas Foundation 2015. © Nam June Paik Estate

Picasso: Accepted by HM Government in lieu of tax with additional payment (Grant-in-Aid) made with assistance from the National Heritage Memorial Fund, the Art Fund and the Friends of the Tate Gallery 1987. © Succession Picasso/DACS, London 2016

Rothko: Presented by the artist through the American Federation of Arts 1969. © 1998 Kate Rothko Prizel & Christopher Rothko ARS, NY and DACS, London

Rechmaoui: Purchased using funds provided by the Middle East North Africa Acquisitions Committee 2010. © artist, 2016, courtesy of the Saatchi Gallery, London

Saint Phalle: Purchased 1984. © The estate of Niki de Saint Phalle

Shimamoto: Presented by the artist 2002. © Shimamoto Shozo

Warhol: Purchased 1980. © 2016 The Andy Warhol Foundation for the Visual Arts, Inc. / Artists Rights Society (ARS), New York and DACS, London

Williamson: Purchased with funds provided by Simon and Catriona Mordant, and the Basil and Raghida Al-Rahim Art Fund, courtesy of Goodman Gallery, 2014. © Sue Williamson

Photographic credits

Photography is © Tate Photography 2016 unless otherwise stated.

Cover photography by Marcus Leith and Andrew Dunkley © Tate Photography 2016

© Hayes Davidson and Herzog & de Meuron 1,3

© Herzog & de Meuron 5 bottom, 42–3

Photo © Ian Kingsnorth 62 right

Courtesy Ana Lupas, photo: Rainer Iglar / Installation at Galerie im Taxispalais / Galerie des Landes Tirol, Innsbruck 53

Courtesy of the Saatchi Gallery, London 59

© Peter Saville, Hayes Davidson and Herzog & de Meuron 44–5

Courtesy Sprüth Magers 31 bottom

Residents Day 2009 © Tate 2

Tate Archives 4

© Tate Photography 2016 / Andrew Dunkley 32, 37 top, 38–40, 49; Andrew Dunkley and Seraphina Neville 8–9; Jo Fernandes 11 top; Mark Heathcote and Rose Hillson Summers .47 bottom; David Lambert 55; Marcus Leith 5 top, 33, 36, 37 bottom, 47 top, 48; Marcus Leith and Andrew Dunkley 24, 50

© Tate Liverpool / Roger Sinek 62 left

Tate is a charity and relies on a large number of supporters – individuals, foundations, companies and public sector sources – to enable it to deliver its programme of activities, both on and off its gallery sites. This support is essential in order for Tate to acquire works of art for the Collection, run education, outreach and exhibition programmes, care for the Collection in storage and enable art to be displayed, both digitally and physically, inside and outside Tate.

For more information, please visit: www.tate.org.uk/join-support

First published 2016 by order of the Tate Trustees by Tate Publishing, a division of Tate Enterprises Ltd, Millbank, London SW1P 4RG www.tate.org.uk/publishing

A catalogue record for this book is available from the British Library ISBN 978 1 84976 316 5

Written by Simon Bolitho, Curator, Interpretation, Tate Modern

Designed by Emma Garnsey

Colour reproduction by DL Imaging Ltd, London

Printed and bound in Italy by Pigini Group – Printing Division, Italy

p.1: Tate Modern, view from the south at dusk (visualisation)